W9-AHU-574

MATH IT!
GUESS IT!

by Nadia Higgins

pogo

Ideas for Parents and Teachers

Pogo Books let children practice reading informational text while introducing them to nonfiction features such as headings, labels, sidebars, maps, and diagrams, as well as a table of contents, glossary, and index.

Carefully leveled text with a strong photo match offers early fluent readers the support they need to succeed.

Before Reading

- "Walk" through the book and point out the various nonfiction features. Ask the student what purpose each feature serves.
- Look at the glossary together. Read and discuss the words.

Read the Book

- Have the child read the book independently.
- Invite him or her to list questions that arise from reading.

After Reading

- Discuss the child's questions. Talk about how he or she might find answers to those questions.
- Prompt the child to think more. Ask: How much time do you estimate it took for you to read this book?

Pogo Books are published by Jump!
5357 Penn Avenue South
Minneapolis, MN 55419
www.jumplibrary.com

Library of Congress Cataloging-in-Publication Data
Names: Higgins, Nadia, author.
Title: Guess it! / by Nadia Higgins.
Description: Minneapolis, MN: Jump!, Inc. [2016]
Series: Math it!
Audience: Ages 7-10. | Includes index.
Identifiers: LCCN 2016007535 (print)
LCCN 2016016180 (ebook)
ISBN 9781620314081 (hardcover: alk. paper)
ISBN 9781624964558 (ebook)
Subjects: LCSH: Rounding (Numerical analysis)–Juvenile literature. | Arithmetic–Juvenile literature.
Classification: LCC QA297.65 .H54 2016 (print)
LCC QA297.65 (ebook) | DDC 513–dc23
LC record available at https://lccn.loc.gov/2016007535

Series Editor: Jenny Fretland VanVoorst
Series Designer: Anna Peterson
Photo Researcher: Anna Peterson

Photo Credits: All photos by Shutterstock except: Getty, 6-7, 8-9, 16-17, 19; Roman Pyshchyk/Shutterstock.com; Thinkstock, 13, 14-15, 16-17.

Printed in the United States of America at Corporate Graphics in North Mankato, Minnesota.

TABLE OF CONTENTS

CHAPTER 1

GOOD GUESS!

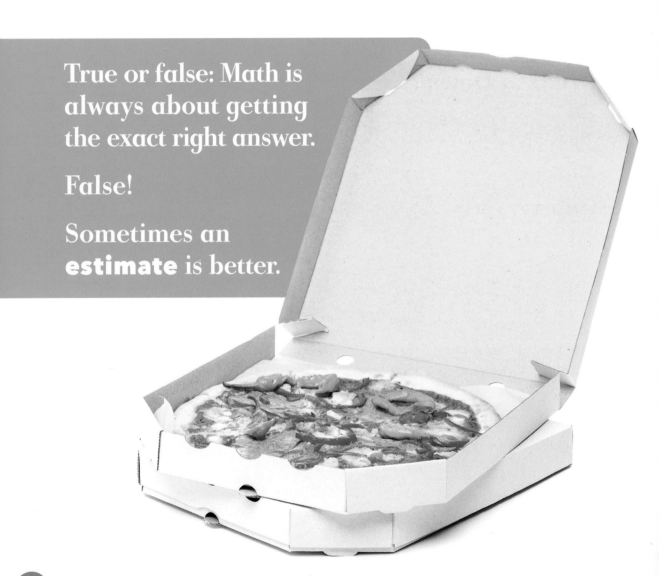

True or false: Math is always about getting the exact right answer.

False!

Sometimes an **estimate** is better.

An estimate is a smart guess. How much pizza will your friends eat? You don't know for sure. But you can guess!

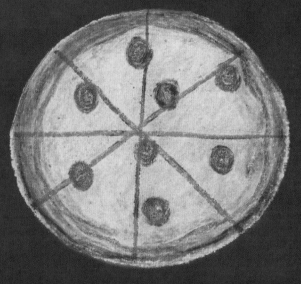

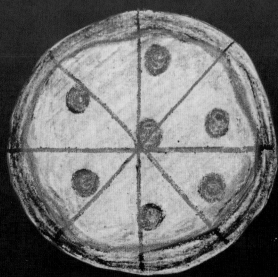

Laura - 2 slices
Judah - 2 slices
Zack - 3 slices
Michelle - 3 slices
Lila - 1 slice
Me - 2 slice

$$2 + 2 + 3 + 3 + 1 + 2 =$$
13 slices

13 slices + a few extra, just in case =
16 slices

order 16 slices!

16 slices = 2 Pizzas

How long will it take
to do your homework?

How many outfits should
you pack for a trip?

You make guesses all the
time about future events.

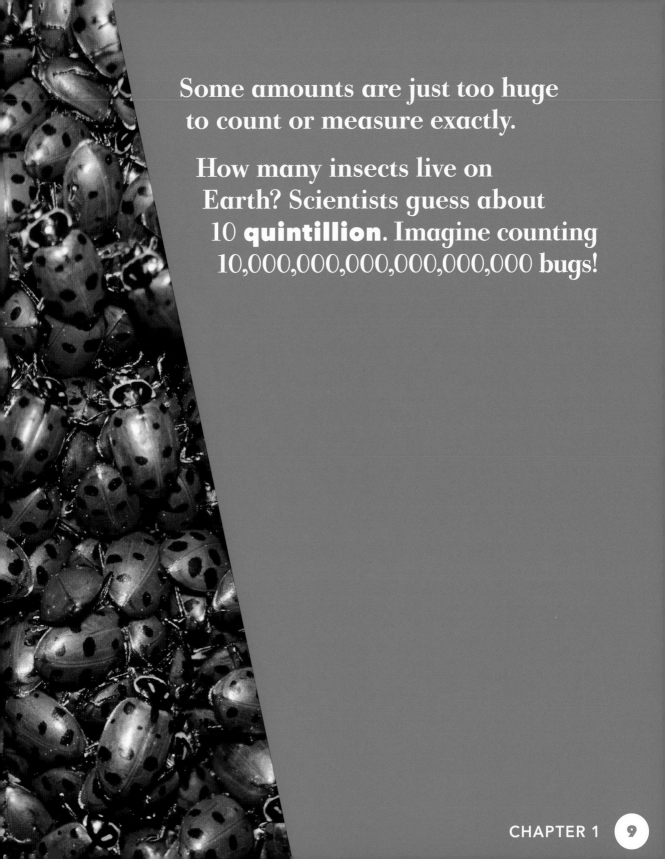

Some amounts are just too huge to count or measure exactly.

How many insects live on Earth? Scientists guess about 10 **quintillion**. Imagine counting 10,000,000,000,000,000,000 **bugs!**

Smart guesses are also a handy way to check answers on a math test.

What is 19 + 33?

Well, 19 is almost 20. And 33 is pretty close to 30.

What's 20 + 30? You can do that math in your head. The answer should be close to 50.

You could have redone every problem on your math test. But that would have taken a long time. Estimation lets you find quick answers.

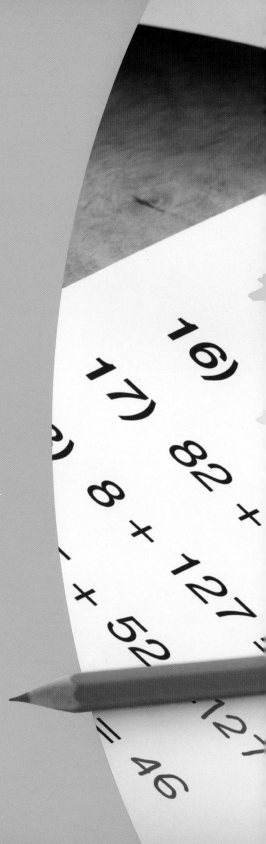

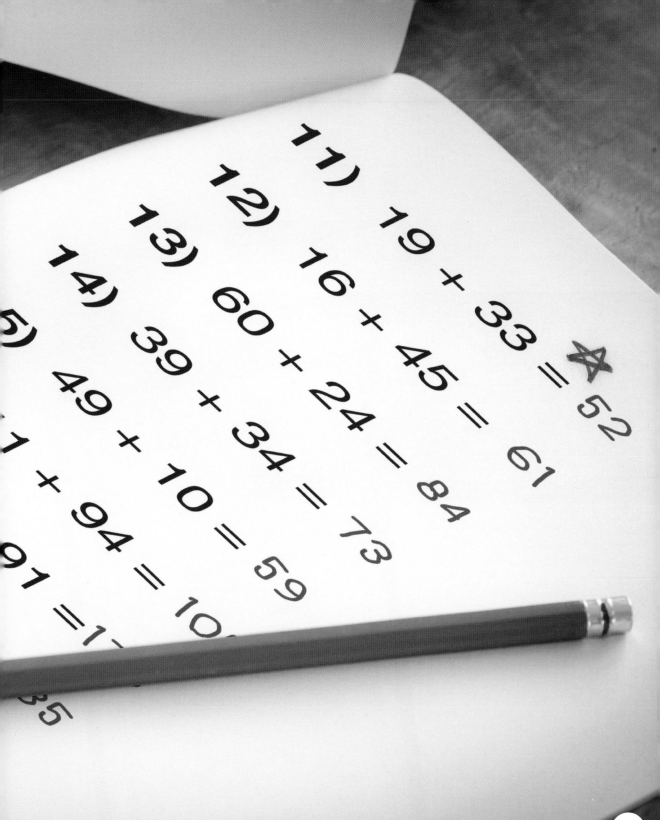

11) 19 + 33 = ⭐ 52

12) 16 + 45 = 61

13) 60 + 24 = 84

14) 39 + 34 = 73

5) 49 + 10 = 59

1 + 94 = 10

91 = 1

35

CHAPTER 2

FAST ANSWERS

You have $10 to spend on lunch.

Quick! Can you afford a cup of soup and a grilled cheese?

LUNCH MENU

SIDES:

French Fries
$5.00

Onion Rings
$5.00

Side Salad
$4.50

Cup of Soup
$2.75

SANDWICHES:

Turkey
$5.75

Egg Salad
$6.25

Ham
$5.75

Grilled Cheese
$5.50

DRINKS:

Coffee
$2.00

Juice
$2.00

Milk
$2.00

Smoothie

Round to the nearest dollar. The soup is about $3. The grilled cheese costs almost $6.

$3 + $6 = $9

You have enough, plus extra for a **tip**.

Which basket of apples
is the better deal?

The bigger basket has 10 apples
for about $10. That comes
out to about $1 per apple.

The smaller basket
has five apples for about
$6 dollars. Don't bother
finding the exact price
of each apple. Is it more
than $1? Yes. At $1 apiece,
five apples would be $5.
This basket costs $6.

The bigger basket
is a better **value**.

How many kids are riding the bus today? Imagine the seats as a **grid**.

Count the rows going up. There are 10.

How many kids fit in each row? Four.

$10 \times 4 = 40$ seats.

This bus is almost full. That means about 40 kids are riding.

THINK ABOUT IT!

What if the bus looked about half full? What would you guess?

· ·

CHAPTER 3

BREAK IT DOWN

What size tank should you buy for your lizard? The tank should be at least three times as long as your pet. That will give him plenty of room to move.

Luckily, you know your lizard is about the same size as your open hand.

Hold your hand up to the tank. Move it along the glass two more lengths. Will your lizard fit? Close enough.

6 blocks × 5 Min
30 minutes

6 blocks × 2 m
12 minu

How long will it take to walk to the park? Let's break down the problem into even **chunks**.

The park is six blocks away. It takes about five minutes to walk each block. That's six blocks at five minutes each.

$$6 \times 5 = 30$$

Your walk will take 30 minutes, give or take.

What else do you want to know? Maybe you don't need to be exact. Just guess!

ACTIVITIES & TOOLS

HOW MANY JELLYBEANS?

Can you guess how many jellybeans will fill a jar? What about paper clips or marbles? See how good you can get at guessing.

What You Need:
- a clear jar
- jellybeans and other different kinds of small objects to fill your jar
- calculator
- paper and pencil

❶ Drop enough jellybeans into your jar to cover the bottom. Count how many jellybeans make one row. Write down your number. For example, 9.

❷ How many rows of jellybeans will it take to fill the jar to the top? Write down your best guess. Let's say 11.

❸ Use a calculator or a pencil to multiply your two numbers. In our example, it will take 11 rows of 9 jellybeans to fill the jar. 11 x 9 = 99. Write down your estimate.

❹ Fill the jar to the top with jellybeans. Then pour them out and count them. (Put them in groups of 10 to make counting easier.) Record your number.

❺ How close was your estimate to the number you counted?

❻ Make more estimates with different objects. Compare your guesses to actual counts. How close can you get?

chunks: Pieces or sections of a whole.

estimate: A smart guess.

grid: A way of dividing something into evenly sized squares.

quintillion: A huge number with 18 zeroes.

round: To substitute an easy number for a hard number that is very close in value.

tip: Money given in thanks to a waiter or another service person for a job well done.

value: How much something is worth compared to how much it costs.

INDEX

TO LEARN MORE

Learning more is as easy as 1, 2, 3.

1) Go to www.factsurfer.com

2) Enter "guessit" into the search box.

3) Click the "Surf" button to see a list of websites.

With factsurfer, finding more information is just a click away.